THE MARATHON CONTINUES

A

IS FOR
ASSET

An ASSET is any resource owned by a person. Anything tangible or intangible that can be owned or controlled to produce positive economic value. The opposite of an ASSET is a Liability.

B

IS FOR
BUDGET

A BUDGET is a financial plan you write down to decide how you will spend your money each month. **A BUDGET** helps you make sure you have enough money every month. **A BUDGET** shows you what money is coming in and what money is going out.

C
IS FOR
CREDIT

CREDIT is the ability to obtain goods or services before payment, based on an agreement that payment will be made at a later time.

D

IS FOR

DEBIT

CARD

A DEBIT CARD is a payment card that deducts YOUR money directly from your checking account. Completely different from a credit card, which is a payment card that is borrowed money that must be paid back in full at the of the month on time.

E

IS FOR

ENTREPRENEUR

An **ENTREPRENEUR** is a person who organizes and operates a business or businesses. An **ENTREPRENEUR** is a market leader because (s)he is the first to start such a kind of enterprise. The **ENTREPRENEUR** is often quite different in mindset from a businessman or manager.

F

IS FOR

FICA

(FEDERAL INSURANCE CONTRIBUTION ACT)

FICA is short for Federal Insurance Contribution Act (not to be confused with FICO). FICA is a US federal payroll tax. It's a contribution directed towards both employees and employers to fund Social Security and Medicare—federal programs that provide benefits for retirees, people with disabilities, and children of deceased workers.

G

IS FOR

GROSS INCOME

GROSS INCOME is your income BEFORE taxes and deductions are taken out.

H

IS FOR

HOME EQUITY

HOME EQUITY is the difference between what you owe on your mortgage and what your home is currently worth.

Ex. If your house is worth 100K and you owe 40K, you have 60K in Home Equity.

IS FOR
INTEREST

INTEREST is the price paid for borrowing money. Normally, expressed as a percentage rate of the money borrowed over a period time.

You can earn or pay interest; it's better to earn.

J IS FOR JOB

A JOB is the work someone does to get paid. A JOB consists of duties, responsibilities, and tasks that are (1) defined and specific and (2) can be measured and rated.

A Career is a series of connected employment opportunities providing experience and learning to fuel your future.

K

IS FOR
KNOW YOUR
CUSTOMER

KNOW YOUR CUSTOMER (KYC) is a process banks make an effort to verify the identity, suitability, and risks involved with a banking relationship. This process helps to ensure banks services are not misused.

Ex. Name, Address, SSN/EIN, Employer

L

IS FOR
LOAN

A LOAN is a type of debt. A LOAN is money, property, or other material goods given to another party in exchange for future repayment of the loan principle amount, plus any interest of finance charges.

There are many different types of loans: personal loan, auto loan, home loan, business loan, etc.

M

IS FOR

MONEY

MONEY most commonly serves as a medium of exchange or means of payment. Including coins and paper money.

In the United States money is referred to as the dollar. However, in different countries money is called something else, looks different, worth a different amount, and sometimes smell different.

NET INCOME is your income AFTER taxes and deductions.

O
IS FOR
OVERDRAFT PROTECTION

OVERDRAFT PROTECTION

is an option offered by your bank that prevents check,ATM, or debit card transactions from causing that accounts balance to fall below zero; incurring an overdraft fee or a non-sufficient (NSF) fee.

P
IS FOR
PASSIVE
INCOME

PASSIVE INCOME is income that require little to no effort to earn and maintain.

IS FOR

QUALIFIED RETIREMENT ACCOUNT

A QUALIFIED RETIREMENT ACCOUNT is a retirement plan recognized by the IRS where investment income accumulates tax deferred.

Ex. Individual Retirement Accounts (IRAs) & Pension Plans

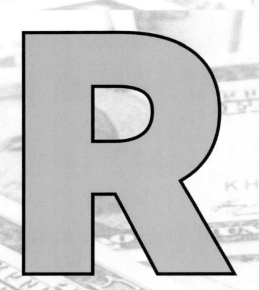

R

IS FOR

RETURN ON INVESTMENT

(R.O.I)

RETURN ON INVESTMENT (ROI) is a financial profitability ratio that calculate the benefit an investor will receive compared to its cost.

ROI is a helpful tool to compare different investment opportunities.

S

IS FOR

SAVINGS

SAVING is the intentional act of setting money aside for a specific goal or purpose.

T

IS FOR

TAXES

TAX is money the government requires people to pay according to their income, their property value, etc. and that is used to pay for things done by the government.

U

IS FOR

UNIFORMED TRANSFER TO MINORS ACCOUNT

(UTMA)

The **UNIFORM TRANSFERS to MINORS ACT (UTMA)** allows a minor to receive gifts — such as money, patents, royalties, real estate, fine art — without the aid of a guardian or trustee.

An UTMA Savings Account is a great tool to save for a child's future.

V

IS FOR

VARIABLE

A VARIABLE is anything that does not have a set value.

*In some cases a variable rate is better than a fixed rate.

W
IS FOR
WEALTH

WEALTH refers to the value of everything a person or family owns.

WEALTH is measured as "net assets"

XD is a symbol used to signify that a security is trading ex-dividend.

It tells investors key information about a specific security in a stock quote.

Y
IS FOR
YIELD

YIELD is the income earned on an investment.

Z

IS FOR

ZERO PERCENT INTEREST

ZERO PERCENT INTEREST

gives you the chance to pay the same amount of money as a cash buyer, even though you're spreading the payments over a longer period of time.

Also known as discounted finance, it is a widely used marketing tool.